WILDERNESS

WILDERNESS

Carolyn Askar

SELECTED POEMS *(1991 - 1998)*

Terracotta Press

*First published in 1998
by
Terracotta Press
(Chincotta)
57 – 63 Line Wall Road
P.O. box 199 & 612
Gibraltar*

ISBN 0 - 9583003 – 0 - 5

Copyright © *Carolyn Askar 1998*
All rights reserved.

*Printed
by
Copycolor
San Pedro de Alcántara
Málaga España*

*Cover photograph: Bryce Canyon, Utah
by
Carolyn Askar*

ACKNOWLEDGEMENTS

to the following publications where some of these
poems first appeared

Envoi; New Spokes; Tenth Muse; Vision On;
Ver Voices; Psychopoetica (Hull University)
and Arrival Press Central Poets anthology

"Timeless Information" is a song lyric from a series recorded
by Pierre Jenni, Switzerland.

and thanks
to Frances Wilson and Riki Gerardy for criticism,
comments and helpful suggestions.

also by Carolyn Askar

***SPIRIT OF FIRE** (Element Books)*
***A UNIQUE CURVE** (Priapus Press)*
***INTERPRETING THE TREE** (Diamond Press)*

Gathering together these poems, various themes began to emerge. The passing of stages of life, growing, ageing and nurturing, seemed to come into a sharper focus. This process was probably accentuated and accelerated by an abrupt change of lifestyle. In March 1994, I left England to travel and live abroad - a very new experience, having been London-based all my life. Observations of places, people and relationships are included here, as well as some poems on gender struggles.

C.J.A.

For my children: Karen Jane, Alexandra and James

CONTENTS

SECTION 1   GLIMPSES IN TIME

Warning	*15*
Ballad of Coombe Martin	*16*
Auntie Hetty's Garden	*18*
Here we go gathering Girls in May	*20*
Feeling Special	*21*
Sisters' Dance	*22*
Strings	*24*
On Mothering	*25*
How long has it been?	*26*
Old Photos	*27*
In Exeter Cathedral	*28*
A Walk before Winter	*29*
Random Glimpses in Time	*30*
Change	*32*
Still There	*33*
Timeless Information	*34*

SECTION 2   ON THE MOVE

On Preparing to Leave	*40*
In this Windowless Oval Room	*42*
Two Faces of Spain	*44*
C.N. Tower - Toronto	*46*
Meat Market - Berber Soukh	*47*
Humming Bird	*48*
Images of Home	*49*

Uncut History	*50*
Rain-forest Spider-woman	*51*
Palenque and Misoljá	*52*
Author´s Note	*54*
In New Mexico	*55*

SECTION 3 EYE TO EYE

Horse	*61*
Parsnip Boy	*62*
Vulnerable Healer	*63*
Cosmetic	*64*
On Fire	*65*
Myope	*66*
In Love?	*68*
A Fantasy	*69*
Proposal	*70*
Not Eye to Eye	*71*
Adam´s Grit	*72*
Like Bitter Chocolate	*73*
Differences	*74*
Shooting the Rapids	*76*
Wilderness	*78*

SECTION 1

GLIMPSES IN TIME

In these poems I have moved freely between early memories and dreams, recent reminders and thoughts on the subject of change, maturing and family/socio- dynamics.

WARNING

In the open mouth of amethyst,
rich crystals glint
through razor-tooth grin.

The inviting sparkle of this cave
belies the sharpness
of the stone

- as the warmth of home
forgets to tell
of fingers
wrapped too closely
round the heart.

BALLAD OF COOMBE MARTIN

Please hold my hand and come with me
down on the beach to follow the sea
as it leaves a playground of pools, where we
can splash, play and explore.

Don't be silly dear, drink your tea.
You don't want to go down there to be
wet and windblown, can't you see
we're better off here indoors.

But I want to go down beyond the quay,
walk right out to where I'll see
and smell fresh seaweed, washed in the lee
of crashing waves on the shore.

But why, when you can sit here and see
it all as clearly as can be
through the window, while we have our tea,
comfortable, warm and secure?

I'll roll my trousers up past my knee,
wade through pools, climb rock and scree,
let waves spray salt all over me,
as I face the wind on the shore.

But it's cold out there, too blustery.
You should be grateful for your nice tea
and the cake and comforts you have here with me,
instead of looking for more.

I want to run and think about me;
I want to find out just who I can be,
breathe sharp air that makes me feel free.
I need to discover more.

Just stop this nonsense! Can't you see
we're all safe here, we're a family.
We can't possibly come with you to the sea.
What are you looking for?

You've always made me sit by your knee,
but now I'll make my own way down to the sea
and on the way, I'll learn about me
and grow, alone, by the shore.

Oh, my child, I begin to see,
you're exactly the way I longed to be,
but I was so frightened, I never broke free.
- Think of me down by the shore.

AUNTIE HETTY'S GARDEN

Someone here cares.
Each leaf and blade of grass
is composted down.

Here there is room for unevenness.

The careful mosaic
of old paving stones,
slots round the rockery,
paths always winding.

Blemished apples and pears
are collected and stored,
baked into spiced cakes
in her fragrant, warm kitchen.

Longing to be lifted to see over the edge
as raindrops fill up the water butt,
I wish the surface nearer the brim.

By the blackberry patch
I stain hands and mouth,
revelling in permission,
glowing with rebellion.

I long to enter the deep communion
I sense between my aunt and her garden,
as it curves and winds, fills and spills
in unregimented rhythm and natural disorder,
where windfalls and hybrids are all accepted.

Now, all these years later,
in my own wild garden,
where roughly-mown lawn
runs into rough pasture
and a tangle of bushes
defines the borders,
I carefully tend
her cuttings of Jasmin
and Lily of the Valley,
given long ago
with love and vision.

HERE WE GO GATHERING GIRLS IN MAY...

*Sunlight dances brazenly
and perfumes rise,
as velvet petals
spread their flounces wide.*

*Flirtatious rose-buds
twist stems self-consciously
and dip heads into shadows,
half-wanting to hide.*

*Lip-sticked in carmine,
some seem to be bleeding,
pricked by the real
thorn in their side.*

*Small white floribunda
cluster close for protection
- nuns pick these for chapel
and shut them inside.*

FEELING SPECIAL
(for Luís)

Longing for attention from either parent,
you retreated into yourself and your closet,
where, in darkness, caressing your dolls,
you imagined marrying an older brother.

I picture you then: a handsome boy,
dusky, delicate, craving affection,
as your five-year-old face was slapped
for showing ' unnatural' yearnings.

As you grew you fought
to harness feelings to gender,
unsuccessfully trying out roles,
clearly modelled for you to follow.
How you must have ached with fear,
quaked in dread of exposing your truth:
feeling yourself a worthless son
who dreamed, like his sisters, of being a bride.

SISTERS' DANCE

Dimity-Doll had big round eyes
and russet apple cheeks.
With her open smile
she rested in love's arms.

Unlike her big sister, Lally,
who was wild. A wayward child,
with knowing look
and darkening frown.

Dimity was always ready to comply,
played 'nurses' with her teddies;
while sister, gun in hand,
was up a tree, trouble-shooting.

In their teens they switched roles.
Dimity, secure, left home,
loved and travelled wide,
seeking and savouring adventure.

Lally chose domesticity:
reproduced and cooked to curry favour;
but found herself gasping for air,
as the web closed tightly round her.

In middle years, they switched again.
Dimity married and had babes:
took up once more her childhood game,
like a duck returning to water.

Lally snipped at apron strings,
and wielding the pen that replaced her gun,
stumbled across an unmarked page
to follow her haunting star.

STRINGS

You were trying to fly your kite.
Helped by your father
you struggled to launch
the enormous two-hander
in uneven gusts.
Too large and heavy
for your twelve years,
it looped and dived
again and again,
while you, frustrated,
stamped the ground.

In a flash I saw you
on the threshold of manhood,
looking back to this day
when the task was too great:
you, defiant, challenging the wind,
determined to launch yourself
from my cradle -
and I cried, in the pause
of this telling moment,
for all the moments
we throw to the wind.

ON MOTHERING

I dreamt I found your horse,
starving in the boot of a car
and I led him out
to feed him with remnants of hay.

I dreamt about finding a cage
full of birds, left to fend for themselves.
I fed them and then let them all fly away.

I had hoped that you, the children,
might one day come back to tend them...

I have watched you grow and go
and have thrown new shoes after you.
Once in a while I slip apples in your bags
(knowing breakfasts never take place)
and when you phone,
to discuss which remedies to choose,
I reach into my cupboard,
piled high with old potions,
then pause and suggest
that you mix your own versions.

But meanwhile, between
the dream and the dreaming,
I find myself guarding,
guarding and polishing
your tidy, empty rooms.

HOW LONG HAS IT BEEN ?

*I remembered Aunt Clara
as buxom, bossy and overpowering.
Now, here I am confronted
by a wizened ninety-two year old,
shrunk child-size.*

*In her eyes,
where the sparkling challenge remains a warning,
I find myself
again the wilful child, lumpy teenager, awkward bride.*

*Enquiring after her close ones
I learn they have dropped from life
without my knowing.
Her son, concerned, fussing,
hovers to see she's well tended.*

*Later,
I wonder about the sentiment
behind her parting statement,
delivered with a smile:*

*"It is nice to see my relatives
- once in a while..."*

OLD PHOTOS

"Smile at the camera",
they used to say,
and for years the expression
adhered to my face
like suctioned polythene
- a tight grimace.

Once or twice, someone
clicked as I looked round,
covered in sand,
or chocolate ice-cream
and captured the child
I might have been.

Even now,
with the practice of years,
I dread a photographer
calling my name
and still feel trapped
when caught in the frame.

IN EXETER CATHEDRAL

"Can you light them for the dead?"
my daughter asked,
as coins fell for our votive candles.
"For the living and the dead", I replied.

Wedging white wax into black sconces,
I found myself placing them in groups
- configurations rising from the past.

As I lit them with their names behind my lips,
I felt their light return to touch my brow
and familiar smiles re-kindled childhood years.

A WALK BEFORE WINTER

*I can tell by the brightness of the sky
in which direction we're headed.
Shadows follow, always at a distance,
but closing.*

*Winding upwards from the stream,
through oaks shedding leaves,
we pause
for the old dog to catch up.*

*Never quite unencumbered,
this natural wait and gather
is as comforting
as the tucking in of bedclothes.*

*As we trudge on through brambles,
we discuss the joy of lanterns:
music, verse and paintings
to brighten twilight days,
and we bend our thoughts round meanings,
subtly woven and tangled.*

*When the dog´s pace becomes our own,
we'll puff slowly up the last hill,
cradling him in our arms
as we begin to fade,
close doors and light our lanterns
for winter.*

RANDOM GLIMPSES IN TIME

1)

*The cactus is bleeding.
Crimson droplets
gather to a finger tip
and drip from the curve
of the wilting flower.
She has had her hour.
No longer tough and strong,
she bends to discover
what she knew all along.*

2)

*In his Chinese coolie hat,
he has been standing for years
with a fish at the end of his line.
Once he was oil-dark and firm as a nut.
Now he is transparent
and his fish is a filigree of bones.
"Dust to dust",
say the passing children,
and his grey smile quivers
with his rod and line
as he watches them
running out of time.*

3)

*Then, from the pool of shadow
that lay across her,
a child rose,
in the shape of a question mark
and danced into the arms
of those who remembered.
These wise ones from the past
gathered up fragments of hope
and forged her a rough pathway
- to the future.*

CHANGE

I catch myself now
sifting women:
pre-menopausal, peri and post.
Their faces a yardstick
for my progression
- where I have come from
where I might go.
I study the fluctuating puffs
and lines that are theirs
but also my own
- on a good day, my daughter
on a bad day, my mother.
Madonna, neutral, crone.

STILL THERE

*Moths do not rise in excitation any more
and kiss is a memory.*

*She can no longer follow the mind
through its maze of splintering tunnels.*

*Purple traces pulse with a sluggish fluid
that barely coats the lining of dreams.*

*Concrete closes round her and weather looms large
as nimbus clouds stuff themselves into her room.*

*Yet still, while a pin-prick of light remains,
a last moth-wing quivers on the rib-cage floor.*

(after visiting the Egyptian Museum in Cairo)

TIMELESS INFORMATION

(Song lyric)

*A king and queen, side by side,
lean into each other's spaces,
carved in stone, painted smile
forever on their faces.*

*Arms around each other's shoulders
for the last five thousand years,
painted eyes still speaking
for their words to reach our ears.*

*/ Listen to the wisdom
of an ancient civilization
our many layered world is filled
with timeless information
- new and timeless
information. /*

*Now icons split apart
crowns and lands asunder
for anarchy to plunder.*

*The past is our future
and our future is the past:
some mysteries hold fast.*

*Across the preparations
for the twenty-first century
ancient, whispered information
renews its plea:*

*/ Listen to the wisdom
of an ancient civilization
our many-layered world is filled
with coded information
- clear and coded
information. /*

(contd.)

*Some mysteries we crack
even through tears,
in spite of our fears.*

*The past is our future
and our future is the past:
some mysteries hold fast.*

*Science and metaphysics
begin to fuse
as planets line up with news.*

*/ Listen to the wisdom
of timeless information,
the mystics hold the key
to transformation.*

*If we dare
transformation,
it's all here -
the information:*

*clear and timeless
information. /*

(written for the music of Pierre Jenni)

SECTION 2

ON THE MOVE

The shifting of perspective is probably one of the most powerful factors in education and in healing - on all levels. I find myself constantly surprised as new places, people and situations produce the most unexpected reactions and responses.

ON PREPARING TO LEAVE
(Autumn, 1993)

*As early frost recedes with the shadows,
we batten down, preparing for winter,
and sweeping up the last of the leaves,
turn away from our nurturing seasons.
Privileged custodians for so many years,
we now let the tools fall from our hands.*

*Patterns too familiar for eyes to register
now sharpen into focus.
The character of each tree, each flagstone,
takes on new significance.*

*Intricate ballets of daily routine
grow heavy with meaning
as each becomes 'the last':
the last crop from the old fig tree;
the last time everyone gathers round this table
in sunlight shafting through rain-smudged windows.*

*Surrounded by the clutter of years,
I must now choose which strings to cut,
steel myself to prioritize
necessity over nostalgia.*

Will blood-ties survive
being stretched to whispers
through satellites and cables
crossing time zones and oceans?

Can letters patch the tears in fabric
painstakingly woven between friends?

Footprints fade fast.
Other hands will close these drawers,
bring in the milk, water my plants.

The ribbon of words
I leave in the dust
will speak to those
I do not know.

*(After Monet's 'Water-Lilies' at L'Orangerie, Paris
- an exhibition designed by the artist to be opened
after his death)*

IN THIS WINDOWLESS OVAL ROOM

*Gaia, I am lost in a sea of stems:
your stems, thickly green beneath the water.
I have waded long through tangled reeds
and smudges of dense colour.*

*Above the surface of my dreams
I see your pink and yellow blooms,
their petals crisp, yet always blurred
and rippling in my eyes.*

*Before me water separates
from land, as slowly I approach
the shadowed margins of the lake
and trees solidify.*

*Beards of willow above the banks
touch their own reflections
and where they meet I find the line
of darkness I can't enter.*

*As white clouds of mystery
gather round my palette's edge
and creep into my canvases,
my vision grows stronger.*

*When I rise from this heavy lake,
where my paint has dappled life,
brush-strokes will live and crystallize
these images around me.*

TWO FACES OF SPAIN
(on observing a gypsy vendor in Andalucía)

"Ah, Señora, you want to buy nice tablecloth?
Look, I sell only finest lace. You like?
You are so beautiful
- and your children, que guapas!
I make you special price, you are my friend,
no? No, wait, please Señora, wait...

What do you know of life,
with your fat sun-tans,
obscene bikinis and elastic morals?
You think you see Spain?
Andalucía is a sangria
in your hotel by the sea?
Your immodesty splashes
like oil off your bellies,
into our clear seas,
clouding, diluting, polluting!

Our rôles have been cut from solid rock
by centuries of cloistered women
and volcanic men.
Behind our walls, fires burn.
Under the biting, white-hot sun,
our passions, fanned by scorching winds,
wait, to explode
in flamenco and matrimonio.

"Ah, Señora, you want to buy nice tablecloth?
Look, I sell only finest lace. You like?
I make you special price, you are my friend,
no? No, wait, please Señora, wait...

*We have seen men with knives
in the dust-brown mountains;
seen blood staining streams
till the arroyos run red
and there is no-one left
to release the white-veiled virgins,
waiting, in the numbing heat,
dry with pain and yearning,
waiting,
till their clothes turn black with mourning.*

Ayaaah... What do you know of life?!"

C.N. TOWER - TORONTO
(in 1992, the world's tallest building)

*From the lakeshore, we rocket up
through a concrete shaft at breakneck speed
and the city recedes, shrinking beneath us.*

*We hover and sway above toy planes,
circling to land on the lake-locked runway.*

*Something compels us, wingless creatures,
to rise above our base perspective,
plant totems to climb and look down upon ourselves.*

*But unlike views from mountain tops,
that fill us and include us in their grandeur,
this dreary structure seems to dwarf our stature,
as we strive to compete with, or imitate nature.*

*And it feels as though Ontario is smiling
at clumsy children's building-blocks and dreams,*

*for through Niagara's horseshoe eye
her mighty tears thunder
and ricochet to spray the clouds
that fall again as rain -*

*reminding us that, one day,
our efforts may be washed away.*

MEAT MARKET - BERBER SOUKH
(Atlas Mountains, Morocco)

A matching set of four,
in shades of brown:
at the base - hooves of bone,
with ankles sawed
to a red fringed crown.

I look for traces of deeper pink
in the puddles on the terracotta ground.

Tangles of fleshy ribbons are piled
on rough wooden boards,
where flies abound.

Curled horns support a sightless face,
still soft with fur, but upside down.
At the neck, a single white pipe, like a shoe-lace,
protrudes from the smooth crimson wound.

The fall from life to table seems more distressing
when we, from the cling-film age,
are confronted
by this lack of window-dressing.

HUMMING BIRD

There you sit:
a thumb-full of life,
sleek silk-feathered,
your exaggerated bill
tapering to a whisker
and fuse-wire feet
gripping a twig.

Here I sit:
three feet away
with camera poised.
We eye each other.

In a moth-wing moment
you whirr your absence of weight
in a flash of green and blue.
My finger is on the button
but there's no time to click
before you dart from view.

- And I wonder how
we clumsy humans
appear to you.

IMAGES OF HOME

"Is that a British accent?"
boomed a Texan voice
in the tiny Taxco courtyard.
"I was in your country...
all those pretty villages...
and of course, I loved the thee-ater."

And through his eyes I see my land
of gentle hills and rich cream teas
in cottages with gardens full of roses;
black cabs and pillar-box buses,
gracious symbols of past splendour,
drifting down a Haymarket lost to time.

Later, in Mexico City,
a friendly young Aztec
enquired where I was from.
"Ah, Inglaterra!" he exclaimed,
"country famous for hooligans!"

And through his eyes I see the press
of angry young faces, trying to carve
a slender portion from left-over dreams,
as they crowd through green, historic hills,
now shrouded in confusing clouds.

UNCUT HISTORY
(observed in Yucatan, Mexico)

*A head of snow
caught at the nape
in a scrap of woven braid.
Grandmother, wise tribal elder.
Below the braid snow melts into cumulus:
rain splashing the sheets
that spread middle-age
across bent back and shoulders.
Did the slow draining of lustre
free her from attentions,
invited by the jet-black flow,
now blanketing the girth
that was once cinched waist?
That distant richness of youth
clings like persistent memory,
softening generations' perspective,
as it fingers down over ample buttocks,
announcing and hiding the past.*

*Tattered curtains of childhood
tap at the back of the knees,
torn shreds like loose shutters
flapping in distant dreams:
when forests covered the land
and underground rivers swelled
to swallow up virgins at Chichen Iza
and the future was ripe with promise.*

RAIN-FOREST SPIDER-WOMAN

She has spread her net
between branches
where it glistens in a shaft
of sunlight through leaves.

Now centred in her symmetry,
she stretches to her extremities,
poison hidden in her silken confection.

She waits and eyes
the potential of punters,
who pause to admire
the shimmer of her gossamer.

(after a visit to the Mayan ruins and the mountains of Chiappas, between Mexico and Guatemala)

PALENQUE and MISOLJA

*Bleached of life, they protrude
like uncovered bones,
wrenched from the clutches
of strangling vines,
roots of trees, sediment of time.*

*Above sealed vaults and tombs of kings
rise excavated temples,
etched with symbols
of earth and sister planets,
mathematically placed
to trace the years.*

*They serve to remind us
of crushed skulls
and hearts of infants: offerings
to the spirit of the jaguar,
to the gods of wind and rain.*

*But the forest keeps returning,
rooting into stone
and greening over pyramids,
again and again.*

*****

Higher in the hills,
a natural temple rises:
Misoljá, tribute to its creator -
God of wind and rain.

Gracefully it tips
clear water from great height,
sculpting land beneath
into a bath fit for gods.
Niches with streams
and wild vegetation
are altars, on which
to offer libations -
not of child's blood,
but of flowing spirit.

Here, each individual,
high priest of himself,
is baptised in a pool
of sublime design.

(From - Poems from the U.S., October, 1997)

Author's Note:

My mother (who died in November 1995) used to to fantasize that the trees, running in a line along the top of the Sierra Palmitera in Andalucia, were American Indians watching the wagon trains pass through the valley.

On the flight between Washington D.C. and Salt Lake City, a stream of imagery, representing the female line in my family, came to me quite spontaneously. My great-grandmother (a midwife) was a lake high in the mountains; my grandmother (a musician) was a cataract flowing from her; my mother a meandering river; and so on.

Little did I realise then how much the themes of mother, ancestry, goddess and black madonna would dominate the women's art/creativity retreat I had signed up for in Albuquerque! But first came a two-week exploration, from the canyons of Southern Utah through The Rockies, over the great divide and on down the Rio Grande valley to Albuquerque - whence the following.

IN NEW MEXICO

1)

Mother, how you tracked me down,
propelled and led me over these mountains,
warming me with your glow of red rock,
pricking my vision with pines and aspens
showering leaves of burning lemon,
quenching my thirst in your deep canyons.

If only your arms could have wrapped me round
as this landscape does now - holding us both.

Back at home in the half light of London,
it was never easy to find you,
often wrapped in fogs of the past.
Nimbus clouds shadowed your eyes
as you tried to find repose in Earth's cradle.
You were not rocked in the waters of spirit.

Yet here, for days we've travelled together,
embraced by unending natural beauty.
We followed the rhythms of ancient drumming
and visions of buffalo and cowboy,
till coming to rest, in Albuquerque -
when you died again and left, in my dream.

2)

So there I fashioned you in clay,
wrapped you round in a clay cradle-boat
and blessed you for your onward journey,
whilst I paused to dig new ground,
among sisters who supported my searching,
as I prepared new words for planting.

3)

Into this landscape
into this sunlight
let the spirit escape.
Over these mountains
into these canyons
into the earth,
delving deep,
scooping and scraping
deeper and deeper,
retrieving the essence
of ancient selves:
revealed as birds,
badgers and wolves;
revealed as woman,
mother and crone;
revealed at last
as the face in the lake.

4)

*So I opened my eyes and senses wider
hoping for the flow of wisdom.*

*Just as vapour rises, when clouds gather,
drenching the land in cascades and torrents,
I received warm rain and overflowed,
dissolving boundaries of self and other
- nations and Earth
- self and life.*

5)

*From within the spiral,
within the gourd,
within the egg
within the womb,
lives spin out
weaving the story,
weaving the dance
of paths that lead home.
Exploring dimensions
of bees, of bulls,
of black madonnas,
crow and faun,
crown and sceptre,
lion and goddess -
voices within
the crypt and the tomb.*

SECTION 3

EYE TO EYE

A view of characters and the constantly shifting, delicate balance of relationships - and how we adapt, or don't adapt, to change.

HORSE

From you, Father, I have received
the steadfastness of your equine nature.
Your measured pace, ordered mind
and polished hooves will still pass muster.

Though your saddle bags were laden at times
beyond endurance, you never stumbled,
faltered, fell or lost that fixed point
that braced your shoulders and gave you strength
not to buckle at each new burden.

With nose to the ground, you plodded on,
rarely daring to raise your gaze
to embrace the geometrical order
of your chosen channel for refreshing spirit:
shared carved trough of blessed water,
Masonic ritual of thirst quenched in stone.

PARSNIP BOY

*Bone-thin,
with salt-streaked, grey skin,
a 'parsnip' of a boy,
legs crossed at the ankles,
waits for his mother
in the winter twilight.*

*Grey wool socks
bag round his ankles
and his knuckly knees
rub themselves together,
mirroring the restless
kneading of his hands.
His eyes, etched round
with hollow circles,
peer through the darkness,
every inch of him straining
towards the car that never comes.*

*This seven-year-old
waits here every day:
alone in the car-park,
raking the road
with the holes of his eyes,
wriggling in his uniform,
not quite understanding
- or unable to accept
that he is a 'boarder' now.*

VULNERABLE HEALER

He collects them like cats,
limping and disfigured,
or simply unable to defend themselves.

With Christ-like patience,
he holds the grazed, the frail,
smoothing their fur and cauterizing wounds.
He enters their stories,
reflecting tortured moments
with the upturned eyes
of a mediaeval icon.

One can lean into his understanding;
trusting in the knowledge that, for him,
impediments are not just acceptable,
but essential and endearing.

From fathomless depths of his own past suffering,
his voice flows in a soothing stream.
It swirls round his rock of personal endurance,
which sometimes protrudes
enough for him to speak of:
imprisonment, torture and solitary confinement,
gruelling, yet scented with a fragrant martyrdom,
paving the way for South Africa today.

COSMETIC
(for Jane)

"Those are P.T.s",
said the lady from Los Angeles.

I followed her gaze
to pink nylon, straining
over twin buoyant bulges.

"It's blue ice, you know."
She continued to inform me
how nipples are slit to insert the foam,
producing the extraordinary
hard round bounce.

I imagined them taking off on their own
- helium balloons
released from their moorings.

"But how can one hunt
for the dreaded lump
in those solid-packed bumps ?"
I enquired.
"Aye, there's the rub", she admitted.

We winced and hugged ourselves,
glad of the sag,
content with our ageing,
naturally imperfect,
non-Plastic Tits.

ON FIRE

*She is on fire and cannot find
a container for her flames.
This passion, not now sexual,
is probably a residue of youthful denial.*

*Flames leap in over-generous gestures;
words stick in a web of under-learnt language;
while colour and form ravel themselves
into a statement through clothes.
Music feeds the fire and simultaneously
subdues raw heat into a steadier flow.*

*There is so much to unlearn.
At times she despairs
of her programmed responses,
as their out-dated clinker
clogs the chimney of her furnace.*

*But when a burglar surprised her,
his intrusion ignited
her keg of stored fuel.
She attacked and knocked him flat,
leaving herself reeling
in shock at the recognition
of her unacknowledged power.*

MYOPE

A small man, stretched tight to snapping point,
his neat stature is always encased
in dapper little suits of narrow beliefs.

Art appreciation, for example,
should be restricted to designs on currencies.
People are measured by financial weight.

Theatre is drama of his own making.
Within the safety of the family arena,
he always likes to play the lead,
manipulating puppets with strings of a purse
to which he alone holds the keys.

Creativity's considered a toy for children
and literature lives in unopened, tooled leather.
Religion should always be ostentatious:
dissenters should pretend, or else be beaten
into conspicuous, guilty submission.

When he gives, he remembers
the cost of the gift and his empty pocket
for years to come.

*He projects his own values on all he meets
and barbed remarks fly in regular salvos.
His venomous hiss is always laced
with a thin syrup of nervous laughter.
The smell of his fear
could asphyxiate a crowd.*

*A gambling man,
he tries to ensure he always wins.
The final card he keeps up his sleeve
is a sharp pain in the chest.*

IN LOVE ?
(for Lizzie in her forties)

Unseen fish
quiver in the rivers of gold.
Rivers of gold
course through her fluted glass.
The glass fills
and spills a waterfall of fins.

One by one her filaments respond,
as gentle brushing startles fronds.
Sea anemones open
and widen on the tide,
that sweeps her fear before it
and breaks in waves,
crashing round her heart.

Peeled layers lie in shreds at her feet,
past wounds healing
as the golden balm flows through her,
newly awakened.

The secret blue cowrie
glows lilac and pink,
compelling,
its pulse can't be ignored

- and every part of her now leaps
in response to the 'phone.

A FANTASY

We could enter into
the magic of the wood
and web ourselves in camouflage of vines.

There, in the shadows
we could talk life through,
excavating roots and exploring branches
to celebrate the writing on the leaves.

With fear and guilt lurking in the leafmould,
we'd drift on the blossoms of our dreams.

We could be as children:
enjoying play, admiring
the way we slot together,
thought to thought,
palm to heart,
balm to hurt
and time just to be still;
each curled alone in synchronized weaving
of alternative scenarios and seasons.

Meanwhile you continue
to live in your cave
and I at the top of my hill.
But once in a while,
under secretive leaves,
can we whisper and play with the moon...?

PROPOSAL

*When you dotted the 'i's that I'd dreamed of
and slipped in some extra vowels,
my language was complete.*

But how could I write it out?

*Would you lend me your pen
and trust that I'd never misuse it?*

*Could I trust you
with the secrets of my pages?*

*Somewhere under the volumes
of close-written lines from our texts,
there must be a clean sheet of paper
we could write on.*

NOT EYE TO EYE
(a vexed villanelle)

You choose to see the angle of my breast
Rather than look me in the eye -
Unused to the customs of the west.

I could respond to this sexist test
With superficial banter, witty and wry.
You choose to see the angle of my breast.

Should I seek to deflect you with a jest
As you dart me looks, predatory and sly,
Unused to the customs of the west?

Despite the message from the way I'm dressed
(these straight-line, loose-fit jackets that I buy)
You choose to see the angle of my breast.

You think my femininity's repressed
(since I don't simper, flirt or show a thigh)
Unused to the customs of the west.

By now, though, I thought you would have guessed:
You're really just not my kind of guy.
You choose to see the angle of my breast -
Unused to the customs of the west.

ADAM'S GRIT

*I am Eve,
but I don't know who invented
that myth about the rib.
It was a small bright opal
of thought that I sprang from.
Bone-hard, determined,
it settled under soft curves
and held its granite against the wash
of aeons of indoctrination.*

*This opal, like a bird,
every so often
beats its wings against the bars of me,
cries out in the night with its choking song,
that moves beyond staves
and quivers to a dissonant
symphony of fire.*

*But the flames rise in a dangerous grate,
where grey cats sit,
with unsinged fur standing on end.
Their red eyes smoke as they watch for birds
who dare weave song-webs strong enough
to challenge their authority.*

*Yet, even so, something
is rising above them,
mellifluously.*

LIKE BITTER CHOCOLATE

*Illusive yet present,
the voice has an essence
like bitter chocolate.*

*It hovers round the ear,
while aural antennae
register the aroma.*

*Moving downwards,
the salty sweetness
stimulates and tantalizes.*

*Rich and darkly smooth,
a tang of humour
trips across the after-taste.*

*A moment to savour,
subtle, then gone
in the click of a 'phone,*

*snapping cold apart,
leaving a sharp edge
and,
like bitter chocolate,
leaving you craving more.*

DIFFERENCES

Like a mocking serpent
you rose in my path
as my dream rattled down
its night-time track.

Daily, on waking,
I heaped stones upon you.
But once in a while
you slithered out
to catch me off guard.

I had grazed the soft skin
I had mistaken for scales.
Had I simply imagined
there was venom in the coils?

As months passed between us
the distance widened
and the pebbles I had piled
built walls of silence.

Yet still your yardstick
would rise before me
challenging me
to reconsider directions.

*****

Now I picture you, sleeping
under a tree
and feel sure, if your thoughts
turn towards me
you flick your tail
to brush them away.

And I've buried the path
that could have led me
back to ask you
for a clearing of the debris.

I wish that quietly,
stone by stone,
we could lay our fears to rest
and build a bridge
across our differences.

(Instructions received in Costa Rica for

SHOOTING THE RAPIDS

struck me as appropriate for applying to life generally)

*The secret is
to aim at the rocks,
then let the current
carry you round.*

*Stay with the flow,
use the river's power
to keep midstream
where the way is clearer.*

*When waves engulf
and spray blinds eyes,
simply hold steady
to keep afloat.*

*Focus on ripples
just in front,
don't fret about possible
plunges ahead.*

*Hold oars tight,
minute adjustments
one stroke at a time,
for swerving precision.*

*Don't look too deep
beneath the surface
where all the worst
scenarios lurk.*

*Never look back,
you could lose direction.
Analyse later,
when on flat water.*

*And if you fall in,
don't struggle to swim.
Stay in foetal position
and trust life to hold you.*

*Ride the water,
don't fight against nature.
Aim at the rocks
and coast with the flow.*

WILDERNESS
(For Huly)

1)
*It is only when I throw away the maps
that I can begin to find my way.*

*Of course, the road had to lead inwards;
I can only write from the inside out.*

*On returning to the kernel of a poem,
I discover the connections
for which I´ve been searching.*

*Only within the inner stillness
can the quickening be felt
and the light explode.*

*In that flash I look back
down the path behind me
with amazement and gratitude for the journey -*

*A journey like labyrinths
we've walked in cathedrals:
when we appear to be moving forwards,
tantalisingly nearing the centre
and tracks double back the way we've come,
but on parallel paths
that shift perspective;*

*tracing patterns that symbolize
the years we wander in the wilderness.*

*****

2)
The sea laps at our back door,
gulls hover and wagtails skim the beach
that stretches wild, for miles.
It draws out my soul,
expanding horizons beyond the point in Africa
that marks the line on a clear day.

Images gather behind our house:
words slip in runnels along the shore
and skim the lapping waves.
I cannot always reach them,
before pebbles slip beneath my feet,
or distractions suck me under.

Here, clean air allows the voice to rise
unimpeded, from the well of oneness
that sings unheard
beneath the daily babble.
And I fly on that song
out and beyond this sea and all oceans.

(contd.)

*****

3)
Our front door is a tall metal gate
that leads to the street.
Through it, at times, I dread to pass,
fearing to meet those with whom
I share no common language.

At times it is hard
to dwell in the chattering world:
to feel myself physically
tugged from my centre,
into a market place
where no one is inspired,

by lapping waves and phrases,
or the sky as it turns
through its fiery transformations.

But you and I, who understand each other,
can enter, side by side, yet separately,
that silent space,
where angels reach inside us
to retrieve the lost child.

Then, lifted into clarity,
a glimpse of home and where we belong
floods us with passion,
fuses dreams with life
and spills visions across a page.

.....